PRO BASKETBALL RECORDS
A GUIDE FOR EVERY FAN

BY MATT CHANDLER

COMPASS POINT BOOKS
a capstone imprint

Compass Point Books are published by Capstone
1710 Roe Crest Drive, North Mankato, Minnesota 56003
www.mycapstone.com

Editorial Credits
Lauren Dupuis-Perez, editor; Sara Radka, designer; Eric Gohl, media researcher;
Laura Manthe, production specialist

Library of Congress Cataloging-in-Publication Data
Library of Congress Cataloging-in-Publication data is available on the Library of
Congress website.

ISBN 978-1-5435-5460-1 (library binding)
ISBN 978-1-5435-5932-3 (paperback)
ISBN 978-1-5435-5465-6 (eBook PDF)

Photo Credits
Getty Images: Allsport, 32 (top), Andy Lyons, 16 (top), Brian Bahr, 48 (top), Erik
Pere, 48 (bottom), Gregory Shamus, 42, Harry How, 4, iStockphoto/blueskyline,
background, Jason Miller, 38, Otto Greule Jr, 13 (bottom), Stephen Dunn, 16 (bottom),
37, 52 (bottom), Streeter Lecka, 29 (bottom), Tim DeFrisco, 28; Newscom: Ai Wire/
Karl Crutchfield, 31, 60 (bottom), Cal Sport Media/Marin Media, 51, Cal Sport Media/
Ron Waite, 55 (bottom), EFE/Todd Pierson, 20 (top), Icon SMI/Darrell Walker, 55
(top), Icon SMI/John W. McDonough, 11, 20 (bottom), 33, Icon SMI/Manny Millan,
27 (bottom), Icon SMI/Matt A. Brown, 35, Icon SMI/TSN, 15 (top), Icon Sports Media,
9, Icon Sportswire/Brian Rothmuller, 10, 46, Icon Sportswire/M. Anthony Nesmith,
54, 58, Icon Sportswire/Stephen Lew, 43 (bottom), Icon Sportswire/Tony Quinn, 57
(bottom), 61 (bottom), Icon Sportswire/Torrey Purvey, 30 (bottom), Icon Sportswire/
Williams Paul, 59, Image of Sport, 12, John McDonough/Icon SMI, 53 (bottom), KRT,
26, 50, 57 (top), KRT/Harry E. Walker, 22 (top), KRT/Jim Prisching, 18 (bottom), KRT/
Nuccio Dinuzzo, 7, KRT/Philadelphia Inquirer/Ron Cortes, 52 (top), Lipofsky.com,
30 (top), MCT/Charlotte Observer/Jeff Siner, 40, MCT/Chuck Meyers, 56, MCT/Fort
Worth Star-Telegram/Jeffery Washington, 24, MCT/Harry E. Walker, 61 (top), MCT/
Orange County Register/Michael Goulding, 17, San Antonio Express-News/Jerry Lara,
43 (top), SIPA/Chine Nouvelle/Qi Henge, 53 (top), SportsChrome/Vince Manniello,
13 (top), TNS, 29 (top), TNS/Akron Beacon Journal/Leah Klafczynski, 44, TNS/Bay
Area News Group/Nhat V. Meyer, 6, TNS/Detroit Free Press/Kirthmon F. Dozier, 14
(bottom), TNS/Miami Herald/Al Diaz, 47, UPI, 23 (bottom), ZUMA Press/Detroit
News/Kirk Dozier, 34, ZUMA Press/Osports, 32 (bottom), ZUMA Press/Sacramento
Bee/Randy Pench, 14 (top), 45, ZUMA Wire/Bildbyran, 8, ZUMA Wire/Chuck
Meyers, 60 (top), ZUMA Wire/Steve Lipofsky, 15 (bottom), 22 (bottom); Shutterstock:
Kanjanee Chaisin, cover; Wikimedia: basketballphoto.com/Steve Lipofsky [http://
basketballphoto.com/NBA_Basketball_Photographs.htm], 25, Eric Kilby, 49, Keith
Alliso, 27 (top), Sport Magazine Archives, 23 (top), The Sporting News Archives/Frank
Bryan, 21, Unknown, 19, World Telegram/Fred Palumbo, 18 (top)

All NBA stats are through the 2017–18 regular season and following postseason. All
WNBA stats are through the 2017 regular season and postseason.

Printed in the United States of America.
PA76

Table of Contents

RECORDS FROM THE COURT

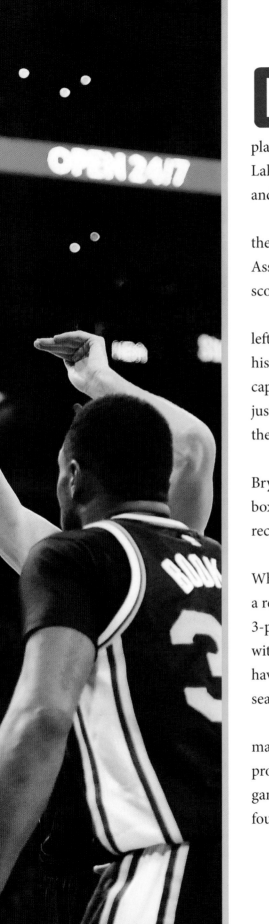

On April 13, 2016, 18,997 fans packed the Staples Center in Los Angeles to say goodbye to a superstar. Kobe Bryant was playing the final game of his 20-year career as a Laker. The fans wanted to be part of his final game and ended up witnessing a record-setting night.

The Lakers guard dropped 60 points on the Utah Jazz. This set a National Basketball Association (NBA) record for the oldest player to score 60-plus points in a game.

With his team trailing the Jazz by 10 and 2:30 left on the clock, Bryant took over. He scored 15 of his team's final 17 points. With 33 seconds left, he capped the comeback by breaking free for a jumper just inside the three-point arc. This gave the Lakers the lead, 97-96.

After being fouled in the closing seconds, Bryant stepped to the line with 58 points in the box score and drained both free throws to set the record and close out a Hall of Fame career.

Basketball is a game built on numbers. Whether it was Dennis Rodman leaping to collect a rebound off the glass or Steph Curry draining 3-pointers effortlessly, the record books are filled with the best players in the game. Some may have had one incredible night, others a dominant season. Some, like Bryant, had an incredible career.

These are the players and teams that have made the NBA one of the most popular leagues in professional sports. Check out the legends of the game as well as today's superstars. They have each found their own spot in basketball's record books.

CHAPTER 1

Player Records

The NBA is a physical game, with players driving the lane and banging bodies in the paint to score. Nothing gets a crowd on its feet like a thunderous slam dunk. But not everyone likes to get dirty inside.

Golden State Warriors guard Steph Curry has been unstoppable from behind the three-point arc. Curry holds the record with four of the top five seasons all-time for three-point shots made. But it was his electric 2015–16 season that tops the record books.

On April 13, 2016, against the Memphis Grizzlies, Curry led his team with 46 points in a 125-104 win. But it was three of those 46 points that were so magical. Less than a minute into the third quarter, Curry cut to the right side of the court. He caught a quick pass from Andrew Bogut. Then, with Grizzlies forward Matt Barnes contesting the shot, Curry effortlessly dropped his 400th 3-pointer of the season.

To be great, a player doesn't have to dominate every part of the game. Some players are incredible shooters. Others live to grab rebounds. Then there are the players who are money from the free-throw line. There are a lot of ways to land in the record books. These NBA greats all found a way.

Most Points

1	Kareem Abdul-Jabbar	38,387	Bucks/Lakers	1969–1989
2	Karl Malone	36,928	Jazz/Lakers	1985–2004
3	Kobe Bryant	33,643	Lakers	1996–2016
4	Michael Jordan	32,292	Bulls/Wizards	1984–1993, 1994–1998, 2001–2003
5	Wilt Chamberlain	31,419	Warriors/76ers/Lakers	1959–1973
6	Dirk Nowitzki	31,187	Mavericks	1998–2018*
7	LeBron James	31,038	Cavaliers/Heat	2003–2018*
8	Julius Erving	30,026	Squires/Nets/76ers	1971–1987
9	Moses Malone	29,580	Stars/Spirits/Braves/Rockets/76ers/Bullets/Hawks/Bucks/Spurs	1974–1995
10	Shaquille O'Neal	28,596	Magic/Lakers/Heat/Suns/Cavaliers/Celtics	1992–2011

* active player

▲ Karl Malone

RECORD FACT

Wilt "the Stilt" Chamberlain averaged 50.36 points per game during the 1961–62 season. His record still stands nearly 50 years later. But scoring isn't everything. Chamberlain's Philadelphia Warriors finished in second place in their division and were eliminated from the playoffs by the Boston Celtics in the Eastern Division Finals.

Most Points

▲ Michael Jordan

SINGLE SEASON

1	**Wilt Chamberlain**	4,029	Warriors	1961–62
2	**Wilt Chamberlain**	3,586	Warriors	1962–63
3	**Michael Jordan**	3,041	Bulls	1986–87
4	**Wilt Chamberlain**	3,033	Warriors	1960–61
5	**Wilt Chamberlain**	2,948	Warriors	1963–64
6	**Michael Jordan**	2,868	Bulls	1987–88
7	**Kobe Bryant**	2,832	Lakers	2005–06
8	**Bob McAdoo**	2,831	Braves	1974–75
9	**Kareem Abdul-Jabbar**	2,822	Bucks	1971–72
10	**Rick Barry**	2,775	Warriors	1966–67

KLAY DAY

Klay Thompson holds the NBA record for most points scored in a single quarter. Facing the Sacramento Kings on January 23, 2015, he put up 37 points in the third quarter, leading his Golden State Warriors to a 126-101 victory.

SINGLE GAME

1	**Wilt Chamberlain**	100	Warriors	Mar. 2, 1962
2	**Kobe Bryant**	81	Lakers	Jan. 22, 2006
3	**Wilt Chamberlain**	78	Warriors	Dec. 8, 1961
4	**Wilt Chamberlain**	73	Warriors	Jan. 13, 1962
	Wilt Chamberlain	73	Warriors	Nov. 16, 1962
	David Thompson	73	Nuggets	Apr. 9, 1978
7	**Wilt Chamberlain**	72	Warriors	Nov. 3, 1962
8	**Elgin Baylor**	71	Lakers	Nov. 15, 1960
	David Robinson	71	Spurs	Apr. 24, 1994
10	**Wilt Chamberlain**	70	Warriors	Mar. 10, 1963
	Devin Booker	70	Suns	Mar. 24, 2017

*active player

Points Per Game

CAREER

1	**Michael Jordan**	30.12	Bulls/Wizards	1984–1993, 1994–1998, 2001–2003
2	**Wilt Chamberlain**	30.07	Warriors/76ers/Lakers	1959–1973
3	**Elgin Baylor**	27.36	Lakers	1958–1972
4	**LeBron James**	27.15	Cavaliers/Heat	2003–2018*
5	**Kevin Durant**	27.12	SuperSonics/Thunder/Warriors	2007–2018*
6	**Jerry West**	27.03	Lakers	1960–1974
7	**Allen Iverson**	26.66	76ers/Nuggets/Pistons/Grizzlies	1996–2010
8	**Bob Pettit**	26.36	Hawks	1954–1965
9	**Oscar Robertson**	25.68	Royals/Bucks	1960–1974
10	**George Gervin**	25.09	Squires/Spurs/Bulls	1972–1986

active player

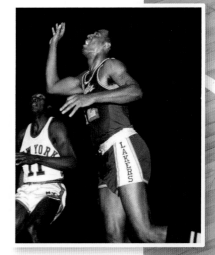

▲ Elgin Baylor

SINGLE SEASON

1	**Wilt Chamberlain**	50.36	Warriors	1961–62
2	**Wilt Chamberlain**	44.83	Warriors	1962–63
3	**Wilt Chamberlain**	38.39	Warriors	1960–61
4	**Wilt Chamberlain**	37.6	Warriors	1959–60
5	**Michael Jordan**	37.09	Bulls	1986–87
6	**Wilt Chamberlain**	36.85	Warriors	1963–64
7	**Rick Barry**	35.58	Warriors	1966–67
8	**Kobe Bryant**	35.4	Lakers	2005–06
9	**Michael Jordan**	34.98	Bulls	1987–88
10	**Kareem Abdul-Jabbar**	34.84	Bucks	1971–72

Field Goal Percentage

▲ Tyson Chandler

CAREER

1	**DeAndre Jordan**	67.26	Clippers	2008–2018*
2	**Tyson Chandler**	59.57	Bulls/Hornets/Bobcats/Mavericks/Knicks/Suns	2001–2018*
3	**Dwight Howard**	58.25	Magic/Lakers/Rockets/Hawks/Hornets	2004–2018*
4	**Shaquille O'Neal**	58.23	Magic/Lakers/Heat/Suns/Cavaliers/Celtics	1992–2011
5	**Artis Gilmore**	58.19	Colonels/Bulls/Spurs/Celtics	1971–1988
6	**Mark West**	58.03	Mavericks/Bucks/Cavaliers/Suns/Pistons/Pacers/Hawks	1983–2000
7	**Steve Johnson**	57.22	Kings/Bulls/Spurs/Trail Blazers/Timberwolves/SuperSonics/Warriors	1981–1991
8	**Amir Johnson**	0.5721	Pistons/Raptors/Celtics/76ers	2005–2018*
9	**Darryl Dawkins**	0.572	76ers/Nets/Jazz/Pistons	1975–1989
10	**James Donaldson**	0.5706	SuperSonics/Clippers/Mavericks/Knicks/Jazz	1980–1993, 1994–1995

* active player

RECORD FACT

Field goal percentage is about shooting the easiest baskets. Dunks, layups, and short jumpers have the best chance of going in. There isn't a single player who has led the league in three-point shots in a season or career that is in the top 10 for field goal percentage.

SINGLE SEASON

1	Wilt Chamberlain	72.7	Lakers	1972–73
2	DeAndre Jordan	71.4	Clippers	2016–17
3	DeAndre Jordan	70.97	Clippers	2014–15
4	DeAndre Jordan	70.28	Clippers	2015–16
	Wilt Chamberlain	68.26	76ers	1966–67
6	Tyson Chandler	67.89	Knicks	2011–12
7	DeAndre Jordan	67.57	Clippers	2013–14
8	Artis Gilmore	67.03	Bulls	1980–81
9	Rudy Gobert	66.08	Jazz	2016–17
10	Clint Capela	65.24	Rockets	2017–18

▲ Artis Gilmore

3-Pointers

CAREER

1	Ray Allen	2,973	Bucks/SuperSonics/Celtics/Heat	1996–2014
2	Reggie Miller	2,560	Pacers	1987–2005
3	Jason Terry	2,282	Hawks/Mavericks/Celtics/Nets/Rockets/Bucks	1999–2018*
4	Kyle Korver	2,213	76ers/Jazz/Bulls/Hawks/Cavaliers	2003–2018*
5	Jamal Crawford	2,153	Bulls/Knicks/Warriors/Hawks/Trail Blazers/Clippers/Timberwolves	2000–2018*
6	Paul Pierce	2,143	Celtics/Nets/Wizards/Clippers	1998–2017
7	Stephen Curry	2,129	Warriors	2009–2018*
8	Vince Carter	2,106	Raptors/Nets/Magic/Suns/Mavericks/Grizzlies/Kings	1998–2018*
9	Jason Kidd	1,988	Mavericks/Suns/Nets/Knicks	1994–2013
10	Joe Johnson	1,978	Celtics/Suns/Hawks/Nets/Heat/Jazz/Rockets	2001–2018*

active player

RECORD FACT

Golden State Warriors point guard Steph Curry led the league in three-point shooting for five consecutive seasons, from 2012–13 through the 2016–17 season.

3·Pointers

▲ Ray Allen

1	**Stephen Curry**	402	Warriors	2015–16
2	**Stephen Curry**	324	Warriors	2016–17
3	**Stephen Curry**	286	Warriors	2014–15
4	**Klay Thompson**	276	Warriors	2015–16
5	**Stephen Curry**	272	Warriors	2012–13
6	**Ray Allen**	269	SuperSonics	2005–06
7	**Klay Thompson**	268	Warriors	2016–17
8	**Dennis Scott**	267	Magic	1995–96
9	**James Harden**	265	Rockets	2017–18
10	**James Harden**	262	Rockets	2016–17

SINGLE GAME

1	**Stephen Curry**	13	Warriors	Nov. 7, 2016
2	**Kobe Bryant**	12	Lakers	Jan. 7, 2003
	Donyell Marshall	12	Raptors	Mar. 13, 2005
	Stephen Curry	12	Warriors	Feb. 27, 2016
5	**Dennis Scott**	11	Magic	Apr. 18, 1996
	J.R. Smith	11	Nuggets	Apr. 13, 2009
	Stephen Curry	11	Warriors	Feb. 27, 2013
	Deron Williams	11	Nets	Mar. 8, 2013
	Klay Thompson	11	Warriors	Jan. 23, 2015
	Kyrie Irving	11	Cavaliers	Jan. 28, 2015
	Stephen Curry	11	Warriors	Feb. 3, 2016
	Stephen Curry	11	Warriors	Feb. 1, 2017

3-Point Percentage

CAREER

1	**Steve Kerr**	45.4	Suns/Cavaliers/Magic/Bulls/Spurs/Trail Blazers	1988–2003
2	**Hubert Davis**	44.09	Knicks/Raptors/Mavericks/Wizards/Pistons/Nets	1992–2004
3	**Drazen Petrovic**	43.74	Trail Blazers/Nets	1989–1993
4	**Stephen Curry**	43.63	Warriors	2009–2018*
5	**Jason Kapono**	43.36	Cavaliers/Bobcats/Heat/Raptors/76ers/Lakers	2003–2012
6	**Kyle Korver**	43.14	76ers/Jazz/Bulls/Hawks/Cavaliers	2003–2018*
7	**Tim Legler**	43.12	Suns/Nuggets/Jazz/Mavericks/Warriors/Wizards/Warriors	1989–2000
8	**Steve Novak**	43.01	Rockets/Clippers/Mavericks/Spurs/Knicks/Raptors/Jazz/Thunder/Bucks	2006–2017
9	**Steve Nash**	42.78	Suns/Mavericks/Lakers	1996–2014
10	**B.J. Armstrong**	42.5	Bulls/Warriors/Hornets/Magic	1989–2000

active player

▲ Steve Kerr

SINGLE SEASON

1	**Kyle Korver**	53.64	Jazz	2009–10
2	**Steve Kerr**	52.35	Bulls	1994–95
3	**Tim Legler**	52.24	Bullets	1995–96
4	**Jon Sundvold**	52.17	Heat	1988–89
5	**Steve Kerr**	51.48	Bulls	1995–96
6	**Jason Kapono**	51.43	Heat	2006–07
7	**Detlef Schrempf**	51.38	SuperSonics	1994–95
	Steve Kerr	50.69	Cavaliers	1989–90
9	**Kyle Korver**	49.22	Hawks	2014–15
	Craig Hodges	49.14	Bucks/Suns	1987–88

▲ Kyle Korver

Free Throws

▲ Dirk Nowitzki

CAREER

1	**Karl Malone**	9,787	Jazz/Lakers	1985–2004
2	**Moses Malone**	9,018	Stars/Spirits/Braves/ Rockets/76ers/Bullets/ Hawks/Bucks/Spurs	1974–1995
3	**Kobe Bryant**	8,378	Lakers	1996–2016
4	**Oscar Robertson**	7,694	Royals/Bucks	1960–1974
5	**Michael Jordan**	7,327	Bulls/Wizards	1984–1993, 1994–1998, 2001–2003
6	**Dirk Nowitzki**	7,201	Mavericks	1998–2018*
7	**Jerry West**	7,160	Lakers	1960–1974
8	**Paul Pierce**	6,918	Celtics/Nets/ Wizards/Clippers	1998–2017
9	**LeBron James**	6,862	Cavaliers/Heat	2003–2018*
10	**Adrian Dantley**	6,832	Braves/Pacers/ Lakers/Jazz/Pistons/ Mavericks/Bucks	1976–1991

active player

FREE THROW FAILURE

Andre Drummond holds one record he wishes he didn't. The Pistons guard missed 23 free throws in a single game on January 20, 2016. Warriors guard Steph Curry had missed only 22 free throws for the season.

SINGLE SEASON

1	Jerry West	840	Lakers	1965–66
2	Wilt Chamberlain	835	Warriors	1961–62
3	Michael Jordan	833	Bulls	1986–87
4	Adrian Dantley	813	Jazz	1983–84
5	Oscar Robertson	800	Royals	1963–64
6	Kevin Durant	756	Thunder	2009–10
7	Rick Barry	753	Warriors	1966–67
8	James Harden	746	Rockets	2016–17
9	Oscar Robertson	742	Royals	1965–66
10	Moses Malone	737	76ers	1984–85

▲ Jerry West

Free Throw Attempts

CAREER

1	Karl Malone	13,188	Jazz/Lakers	1985–2004
2	Moses Malone	11,864	Stars/Spirits/Braves/ Rockets/76ers/ Bullets/Hawks/ Bucks/Spurs	1974–1995
3	Wilt Chamberlain	11,862	Warriors/76ers/Lakers	1959–1973
4	Shaquille O'Neal	11,252	Magic/Lakers/Heat/ Suns/Cavaliers/Celtics	1992–2011
5	Kobe Bryant	10,011	Lakers	1996–2016
6	Kareem Abdul-Jabbar	9,304	Bucks/Lakers	1969–1989
7	LeBron James	9,283	Cavaliers/Heat	2003–2018*
8	Oscar Robertson	9,185	Royals/Bucks	1960–1974
9	Dwight Howard	8,837	Magic/Lakers/ Rockets/Hawks/ Hornets	2004–2018*
10	Jerry West	8,801	Lakers	1960–1974

*active player

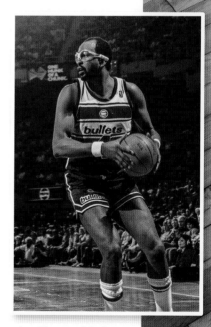

▲ Moses Malone

Free Throw Attempts

▲ Shaquille O'Neal

1	**Wilt Chamberlain**	1.363	Warriors	1961–62
2	**Wilt Chamberlain**	1,113	Warriors	1962–63
3	**Wilt Chamberlain**	1,054	Warriors	1960–61
4	**Wilt Chamberlain**	1,016	Warriors	1963–64
5	**Wilt Chamberlain**	991	Warriors	1959–60
6	**Jerry West**	977	Lakers	1965–66
7	**Wilt Chamberlain**	976	76ers	1965–66
8	**Michael Jordan**	972	Bulls	1986–87
	Shaquille O'Neal	972	Lakers	2000–01
10	**Charles Barkley**	951	76ers	1987–88

MONEY FROM THE LINE

Micheal Williams was a journeyman point guard who played for six teams during an 11-year NBA career. He was as cool as ice from the free-throw line. Williams holds the NBA record for most consecutive free throws made. He drained 97 in a row during a 19-game stretch in 1993.

▶ Michael Williams

Free Throw Percentage

CAREER

1	**Steve Nash**	90.43	Suns/Mavericks/Lakers	1996–2014
2	**Mark Price**	90.39	Cavaliers/Bullets/Warriors/Magic	1986–1998
3	**Stephen Curry**	90.33	Warriors	2009–2018*
4	**Peja Stojakovic**	89.48	Kings/Pacers/Hornets/Raptors/Mavericks	1998–2011
5	**Chauncey Billups**	89.40	Celtics/Raptors/Nuggets/Timberwolves/Pistons/Knicks/Clippers	1997–2014
6	**Ray Allen**	89.39	Bucks/SuperSonics/Celtics/Heat	1996–2014
7	**Rick Barry**	89.31	Warriors/Oaks/Capitols/Nets/Rockets	1965–1967, 1968–1980
8	**Calvin Murphy**	89.16	Rockets	1970–1983
9	**J.J. Redick**	89.00	Magic/Bucks/Clippers/76ers	2006–2018*
10	**Scott Skiles**	88.91	Bucks/Pacers/Magic/Bullets/76ers	1986–1996

active player

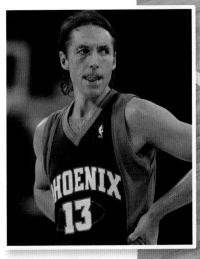

▲ Steve Nash

SINGLE SEASON

1	**Jose Calderon**	98.05	Raptors	2008–09
2	**Calvin Murphy**	95.81	Rockets	1980–81
3	**Mahmoud Abdul-Rauf**	95.63	Nuggets	1993–94
4	**Ray Allen**	95.18	Celtics	2008–09
5	**Jeff Hornacek**	95.00	Jazz	1999–2000
6	**Mark Price**	94.75	Cavaliers	1992–93
6	**Mark Price**	94.74	Cavaliers	1991–92
8	**Rick Barry**	94.67	Rockets	1978–79
9	**Ernie DiGregorio**	94.52	Braves	1976–77
10	**Brian Roberts**	93.98	Pelicans	2013–14

Rebounds

▲ Wilt Chamberlain

CAREER

1	Wilt Chamberlain	23,924	Warriors/76ers/Lakers	1959–1973
2	Bill Russell	21,620	Celtics	1956–1969
3	Moses Malone	17,834	Stars/Spirits/Braves/ Rockets/76ers/Bullets/ Hawks/Bucks/Spurs	1974–1995
4	Kareem Abdul-Jabbar	17,440	Bucks/Lakers	1969–1989
5	Artis Gilmore	16,330	Colonels/Bulls/ Spurs/Celtics	1971–1988
6	Elvin Hayes	16,279	Rockets/Bullets	1968–1984
7	Tim Duncan	15,091	Spurs	1997–2016
8	Karl Malone	14,968	Jazz/Lakers	1985–2004
9	Robert Parish	14,715	Warriors/Celtics/ Hornets/Bulls	1976–1997
10	Kevin Garnett	14,662	Timberwolves/ Celtics/Nets	1995–2016

REBOUNDING FOR RINGS

Dennis Rodman was known as much for his rainbow hair and tattoos as he was for his play on the court. Though he isn't in the top 10 in career rebounds, Rodman was a force on the boards during his career. His 11,954 career rebounds helped his teams earn five NBA titles.

SINGLE SEASON

1	**Wilt Chamberlain**	2,149	Warriors	1960–61
2	**Wilt Chamberlain**	2,052	Warriors	1961–62
3	**Wilt Chamberlain**	1,957	76ers	1966–67
4	**Wilt Chamberlain**	1,952	76ers	1967–68
5	**Wilt Chamberlain**	1,946	Warriors	1962–63
6	**Wilt Chamberlain**	1,943	76ers	1965–66
7	**Wilt Chamberlain**	1,941	Warriors	1959–60
8	**Bill Russell**	1,930	Celtics	1963–64
9	**Bill Russell**	1,878	Celtics	1964–65
10	**Bill Russell**	1,868	Celtics	1960–61

SINGLE GAME

1	**Wilt Chamberlain**	55	Warriors	Nov. 24, 1960
2	**Bill Russell**	51	Celtics	Feb. 5, 1960
3	**Bill Russell**	49	Celtics	Nov. 16, 1957
	Bill Russell	49	Celtics	Mar. 11, 1965
5	**Wilt Chamberlain**	45	Warriors	Feb. 6, 1960
	Wilt Chamberlain	45	Warriors	Jan. 21, 1961
7	**Wilt Chamberlain**	43	Warriors	Nov. 10, 1959
	Wilt Chamberlain	43	Warriors	Dec. 8, 1961
	Bill Russell	43	Celtics	Jan. 20, 1963
	Wilt Chamberlain	43	76ers	Mar. 6, 1965

active player

▲ **Bill Russell**

19

Defensive Rebounds

CAREER

1	**Artis Gilmore**	11,514	Colonels/Bulls/Spurs/Celtics	1971–1988
2	**Kevin Garnett**	11,453	Timberwolves/Celtics/Nets	1995–2016
3	**Karl Malone**	11,406	Jazz/Lakers	1985–2004
4	**Tim Duncan**	11,232	Spurs	1997–2016
5	**Moses Malone**	10,452	Stars/Spirits/Braves/ Rockets/76ers/Bullets/ Hawks/Bucks/Spurs	1974–1995
6	**Robert Parish**	10,117	Warriors/Celtics/Hornets/Bulls	1976–1997
7	**Dirk Nowitzki**	9,868	Mavericks	1998–2018*
8	**Hakeem Olajuwon**	9,714	Rockets/Raptors	1984–2002
9	**Dwight Howard**	9,454	Magic/Lakers/Rockets/ Hawks/Hornets	2004–2018*
10	**Kareem Abdul-Jabbar**	9,394	Bucks/Lakers	1969–1989

active player

▲ Dwight Howard

CHARLES IN CHARGE

Today he is best known for his colorful opinions as a television broadcaster. But as a player, Charles Barkley was a dominant rebounder. "Sir" Charles earned a second nickname, the "Round Mound of Rebounds." Despite his stocky build, Barkley outworked many of his opponents on his way to collecting 12,546 career rebounds.

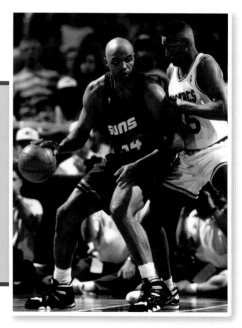

▲ Charles Barkley

SINGLE SEASON

1	**Kareem Abdul-Jabbar**	1,111	Lakers	1975–76
2	**Elvin Hayes**	1,109	Bullets	1973–74
3	**Spencer Haywood**	1,104	Rockets	1969–70
4	**Julius Keye**	1,084	Rockets	1970–71
5	**Mel Daniels**	1,081	Pacers	1970–71
6	**Artis Gilmore**	1,070	Colonels	1971–72
7	**Artis Gilmore**	1,060	Colonels	1973–74
8	**Mel Daniels**	1,039	Pacers	1969–70
9	**Artis Gilmore**	1,027	Colonels	1972–73
10	**Dennis Rodman**	1,007	Pistons	1991–92

▲ Kareem Abdul-Jabbar

SINGLE GAME

1	**Rony Seikaly**	26	Heat	Mar. 3, 1993
2	**Herb Williams**	25	Pacers	Jan. 23, 1989
	Charles Barkley	25	Rockets	Nov. 2, 1996
	Shaquille O'Neal	25	Lakers	Mar. 21, 2004
5	**Dennis Rodman**	23	Spurs	Jan. 22, 1994
	Dikembe Mutombo	23	Nuggets	Mar. 26, 1996
	Tim Duncan	23	Spurs	Feb. 1, 2003
	Kevin Garnett	23	Timberwolves	Dec. 5, 2003
	Kevin Garnett	23	Timberwolves	Jan. 12, 2005
	Al Jefferson	23	Timberwolves	Jan. 13, 2010
	Dwight Howard	23	Lakers	Jan. 6, 2013

stats begin in 1983

Offensive Rebounds

1	**Moses Malone**	7,382	Stars/Spirits/Braves/ Rockets/76ers/Bullets/ Hawks/Bucks/Spurs	1974–1995
2	**Artis Gilmore**	4,816	Colonels/Bulls/Spurs/Celtics	1971–1988
3	**Robert Parish**	4,598	Warriors/Celtics/ Hornets/Bulls	1976–1997
4	**Buck Williams**	4,526	Nets/Trail Blazers/Knicks	1981–1998
5	**Dennis Rodman**	4,329	Pistons/Spurs/Bulls/ Lakers/Mavericks	1986–2000
6	**Charles Barkley**	4,260	76ers/Suns/Rockets	1984–2000
7	**Shaquille O'Neal**	4,209	Magic/Lakers/Heat/ Suns/Cavaliers/Celtics	1992–2011
8	**Kevin Willis**	4,132	Hawks/Heat/Warriors/ Rockets/Raptors/Nuggets/ Spurs/Mavericks	1984–2005, 2006–2007
9	**Hakeem Olajuwon**	4,034	Rockets/Raptors	1984–2002
10	**Charles Oakley**	3,924	Bulls/Knicks/Raptors/ Wizards/Rockets	1985–2004

▲ Charles Oakley

THE "CHAIRMAN OF THE BOARDS"

Moses Malone holds five of the top 10 spots for most offensive rebounds in a season. The NBA Hall of Famer also holds the record for most consecutive seasons leading the league in offensive boards. He led all players in offensive rebounds every season from 1976 to 1983. He capped off the streak by winning the NBA title in 1983 with the Philadelphia 76ers.

SINGLE SEASON

1	Moses Malone	587	Rockets	1978–79
2	Moses Malone	573	Rockets	1979–80
3	Moses Malone	558	Rockets	1981–82
4	Spencer Haywood	533	Rockets	1969–70
5	Dennis Rodman	523	Pistons	1991–92
6	Mel Daniels	502	Muskies	1967–68
7	Artis Gilmore	478	Colonels	1973–74
8	Julius Erving	476	Squires	1971–72
9	Moses Malone	474	Rockets	1980–81
10	Moses Malone	455	Stars	1974–75

▲ Julius Erving

SINGLE GAME

1	Moses Malone	21	Rockets	Feb. 11, 1982
2	Moses Malone	19	Rockets	Feb. 9, 1979
3	Charles Oakley	18	Bulls	Mar. 15, 1986
	Dennis Rodman	18	Pistons	Mar. 4, 1992
	Zaza Pachulia	18	Bucks	Mar. 20, 2015
6	Jayson Williams	17	Nets	Oct. 31, 1997
7	Seven players tied with 16			

▲ Jayson Williams

Assists

CAREER

1	**John Stockton**	15,806	Jazz	1984–2003
2	**Jason Kidd**	12,091	Mavericks/Suns/Nets/Knicks	1994–2013
3	**Steve Nash**	10,335	Suns/Mavericks/Lakers	1996–2014
4	**Mark Jackson**	10,334	Knicks/Clippers/Pacers/Nuggets/Raptors/Jazz/Rockets	1987–2004
5	**Magic Johnson**	10,141	Lakers	1979–1991, 1995–1996
6	**Oscar Robertson**	9,887	Royals/Bucks	1960–1974
7	**Isiah Thomas**	9,061	Pistons	1981–1994
8	**Gary Payton**	8,966	SuperSonics/Bucks/Lakers/Celtics/Heat	1990–2007
9	**Chris Paul**	8,708	Hornets/Clippers/Rockets	2005–2018*
10	**Andre Miller**	8,524	Cavaliers/Clippers/Nuggets/76ers/Trail Blazers/Wizards/Kings/Timberwolves/Spurs	1999–2016

* active player

▲ Jason Kidd

SINGLE SEASON

1	John Stockton	1,164	Jazz	1990–91
2	John Stockton	1,134	Jazz	1989–90
3	John Stockton	1,128	Jazz	1987–88
4	John Stockton	1,126	Jazz	1991–92
5	Isiah Thomas	1,123	Pistons	1984–85
6	John Stockton	1,118	Jazz	1988–89
7	Kevin Porter	1,099	Pistons	1978–79
8	John Stockton	1,031	Jazz	1993–94
9	John Stockton	1,011	Jazz	1994–95
10	Kevin Johnson	991	Suns	1988–89

▲ John Stockton

Steals

CAREER

1	John Stockton	3,265	Jazz	1984–2003
2	Jason Kidd	2,684	Mavericks/Suns/Nets/Knicks	1994–2013
3	Michael Jordan	2,514	Bulls/Wizards	1984–1993, 1994–1998, 2001–2003
4	Gary Payton	2,445	SuperSonics/Bucks/Lakers/Celtics/Heat	1990–2007
5	Maurice Cheeks	2,310	76ers/Spurs/Knicks/Hawks/Nets	1978–1993
6	Scottie Pippen	2,307	Bulls/Rockets/Trail Blazers	1987–2004
7	Julius Erving	2,272	Squires/Nets/76ers	1971–1987
8	Clyde Drexler	2,207	Trail Blazers/Rockets	1983–1998
9	Hakeem Olajuwon	2,162	Rockets/Raptors	1984–2002
10	Alvin Robertson	2,112	Spurs/Bucks/Pistons/Raptors	1984–1993, 1995–1996

"HAVLICEK STOLE THE BALL!"

Perhaps the most famous steal in league history took place in Game 7 of the 1965 Eastern Conference championships. With five seconds left in the game, the Boston Celtics held a one-point lead over the Philadelphia 76ers. The 76ers had the ball with a chance to win. Celtics Guard John Havlicek jumped the inbounds pass and stole the ball. This sent the Celtics to the NBA Finals, where they won the title.

Steals

PLAYOFF THIEF

Allen Iverson earned a spot in the Hall of Fame largely because of his offensive skills. But "The Answer" was a sneaky thief on the court as well. Iverson set the record for most steals in a single playoff game. He swiped 10 balls for the Philadelphia 76ers on May 13, 1999, against the Orlando Magic. The 76ers won the game 97-85—and the series, three games to one.

▲ Allen Iverson

Blocks

CAREER

1	**Hakeem Olajuwon**	3,830	Rockets/Raptors	1984–2002
2	**Dikembe Mutombo**	3,289	Nuggets/Hawks/76ers/ Nets/Knicks/Rockets	1991–2009
3	**Kareem Abdul-Jabbar**	3,189	Bucks/Lakers	1969–1989
4	**Artis Gilmore**	3,178	Colonels/Bulls/Spurs/Celtics	1971–1988
5	**Mark Eaton**	3,064	Jazz	1982–1993
6	**Tim Duncan**	3,020	Spurs	1997–2016
7	**David Robinson**	2,954	Spurs	1989–2003
8	**Patrick Ewing**	2,894	Knicks/SuperSonics/Magic	1985–2002
9	**Shaquille O'Neal**	2,732	Magic/Lakers/Heat/ Suns/Cavaliers/Celtics	1992–2011
10	**Tree Rollins**	2,542	Hawks/Cavaliers/Pistons/ Rockets/Magic	1977–1995

▲ Dikembe Mutombo

▲ Manute Bol and Spud Webb

THE MAGIC OF MANUTE

Manute Bol was a giant at 7 feet 7 inches (231 centimeters) tall. It makes sense that he was a great shot blocker. Bol holds one of the most unusual records in history. He is the only player in the NBA to record more blocks (2,086) than points (1,599) in his career.

Blocks

▲ Mark Eaton

SINGLE SEASON

1	Mark Eaton	456	Jazz	1984–85
2	Artis Gilmore	422	Colonels	1971–72
3	Manute Bol	397	Bullets	1985–86
4	Elmore Smith	393	Lakers	1973–74
5	Hakeem Olajuwon	376	Rockets	1989–90
6	Mark Eaton	369	Jazz	1985–86
7	Mark Eaton	351	Jazz	1983–84
8	Manute Bol	345	Warriors	1988–89
9	Tree Rollins	343	Hawks	1982–83
10	Hakeem Olajuwon	342	Rockets	1992–93

SINGLE GAME

1	Elmore Smith	17	Lakers	Oct. 28, 1973
2	Manute Bol	15	Bullets	Jan. 25, 1986
	Manute Bol	15	Bullets	Feb. 26, 1987
	Shaquille O'Neal	15	Magic	Nov. 20, 1993
5	Elmore Smith	14	Lakers	Oct. 26, 1973
	Elmore Smith	14	Lakers	Nov. 4, 1973
	Mark Eaton	14	Jazz	Jan. 18, 1985
	Mark Eaton	14	Jazz	Feb. 18, 1989
9	Six players tied with 13			

Double Doubles

CAREER

1	**Tim Duncan**	841	Spurs	1997–2016
2	**Karl Malone**	811	Jazz/Lakers	1985–2004
3	**Hakeem Olajuwon**	774	Rockets/Raptors	1984–2002
4	**Kevin Garnett**	741	Timberwolves/ Celtics/Nets	1995–2016
5	**Shaquille O'Neal**	727	Magic/Lakers/Heat/ Suns/Cavaliers/Celtics	1992–2011
6	**Dwight Howard**	719	Magic/Lakers/Rockets/ Hawks/Hornets	2004–2018*
7	**Charles Barkley**	706	76ers/Suns/Rockets	1984–2000
8	**Patrick Ewing**	580	Knicks/SuperSonics/ Magic	1985–2002
9	**David Robinson**	543	Spurs	1989–2003
10	**Pau Gasol**	530	Grizzlies/Lakers/ Bulls/Spurs	2001–2018*

active player

▲ Kevin Garnett

DOUBLE DOUBLE DUNCAN

Tim Duncan spent his entire 19-year NBA career with the San Antonio Spurs. He collected five rings with the Spurs, and a playoff record as well. Duncan tallied 164 double doubles in his postseason career, the most ever.

◀ Tim Duncan

Triple Doubles

▲ Magic Johnson

CAREER

1	**Oscar Robertson**	181	Royals/Bucks	1960–1974
2	**Magic Johnson**	138	Lakers	1979–1991, 1995–1996
3	**Jason Kidd**	107	Mavericks/Suns/Nets/Knicks	1994–2013
4	**Russell Westbrook**	104	Thunder	2008–2018*
5	**Wilt Chamberlain**	78	Warriors/76ers/Lakers	1959–1973
6	**LeBron James**	73	Cavaliers/Heat	2003–2018*
7	**Larry Bird**	59	Celtics	1979–1992
8	**Fat Lever**	43	Trail Blazers/Nuggets/Mavericks	1982–1992, 1993–1994
9	**James Harden**	35	Thunder/Rockets	2009–2018
10	**Bob Cousy**	33	Celtics/Royals	1950–1963, 1969–1970

active player

KING OF THE TRIPLE DOUBLE

On April 9, 2017, Oklahoma City Thunder superstar Russell Westbrook scored 50 points, collected 16 rebounds, and dished 10 assists. But it wasn't just a great game for Westbrook. It was a record breaker—50/16/10 gave Westbrook his 42nd triple double of the season. He broke the mark of 41 set by Oscar Robertson in the 1961–62 season. To give his record some perspective, NBA legend Michael Jordan only tallied 28 triple doubles for his entire career.

▶ Russell Westbrook

Quadruple Doubles

CAREER

To tally double digits in four separate categories in a single game is a rare feat. It has happened only four times in NBA history. Michael Jordan never did it. Neither did Magic Johnson, Larry Bird, or Wilt Chamberlain. Even LeBron James hasn't done it—yet. But these four ballers are in the rarest of NBA air, the quadruple double.

	POINTS	ASSISTS	REBOUNDS			
Nate Thurmond	22	13	14	12 blocks	Bulls	Oct. 18, 1974
Alvin Robertson	20	10	11	10 steals	Spurs	Feb. 18, 1986
Hakeem Olajuwon	18	10	16	11 blocks	Rockets	Mar. 29, 1990
David Robinson	34	10	10	10 blocks	Spurs	Feb. 17, 1994

▲ David Robinson

MVP Awards

#	Player	MVPs
1	Kareem Abdul-Jabbar	6
2	Michael Jordan	5
	Bill Russell	5
4	Wilt Chamberlain	4
	Julius Erving	4
	LeBron James	4
7	Larry Bird	3
	Magic Johnson	3
	Moses Malone	3
10	Stephen Curry	2
	Mel Daniels	2
	Tim Duncan	2
	Karl Malone	2
	Steve Nash	2
	Bob Pettit	2

▲ Larry Bird

MV-KING

LeBron James led his Miami Heat to the NBA title in the 2012–13 season and collected his fourth league MVP award along the way. King James is tied with Wilt Chamberlain and Julius Erving for fourth all-time, with four MVP trophies.

◀ LeBron James

Personal Fouls

CAREER

1	Kareem Abdul-Jabbar	4,657	Bucks/Lakers	1969–1989
2	Karl Malone	4,578	Jazz/Lakers	1985–2004
3	Artis Gilmore	4,529	Colonels/Bulls/Spurs/Celtics	1971–1988
4	Robert Parish	4,443	Warriors/Celtics/Hornets/Bulls	1976–1997
5	Caldwell Jones	4,436	Conquistadors/Sails/Colonels/Spirits of St. Louis/76ers/Rockets/Bulls/Trail Blazers/Spurs	1973–1990
6	Charles Oakley	4,421	Bulls/Knicks/Raptors/Wizards/Rockets	1985–2004
7	Hakeem Olajuwon	4,383	Rockets/Raptors	1984–2002
8	Buck Williams	4,267	Nets/Trail Blazers/Knicks	1981–1998
9	Elvin Hayes	4,193	Rockets/Bullets	1968–1984
10	Clifford Robinson	4,175	Trail Blazers/Suns/Pistons/Warriors/Nets	1989–2007

▲ Robert Parish

SINGLE SEASON

1	Darryl Dawkins	386	Nets	1983–84
2	Gene Moore	382	Colonels	1969–70
3	Darryl Dawkins	379	Nets	1982–83
4	Steve Johnson	372	Kings	1981–82
5	Shawn Kemp	371	Cavaliers	1999–00
6	Gene Moore	369	Conquistadors	1972–73
7	Bill Robinzine	367	Kings	1978–79
8	Bill Bridges	366	Hawks	1967–68
9	James Edwards	363	Pacers	1978–79
10	Lonnie Shelton	363	Knicks	1976–77

A "FOUL" RECORD

"Bubba" Wells only played one season in the NBA, but he still found a place in the record books. Wells earned the distinction of the fastest time in NBA history to foul out of a game. The 6-foot-5-inch (196-cm) small forward committed six fouls in the first three minutes of a game on December 29, 1997, to earn an early shower. He played just 39 games with the Dallas Mavericks that season, and he never played in the NBA again.

Turnovers

▲ Isiah Thomas

CAREER

1	**Karl Malone**	4,524	Jazz/Lakers	1985–2004
2	**Moses Malone**	4,264	Stars/Spirits/Braves/ Rockets/76ers/Bullets/ Hawks/Bucks/Spurs	1974–1995
3	**John Stockton**	4,244	Jazz	1984–2003
4	**Kobe Bryant**	4,010	Lakers	1996–2016
5	**Jason Kidd**	4,003	Mavericks/Suns/Nets/Knicks	1994–2013
6	**LeBron James**	3,966	Cavaliers/Heat	2003–2018*
7	**Julius Erving**	3,940	Squires/Nets/76ers	1971–1987
8	**Artis Gilmore**	3,926	Colonels/Bulls/Spurs/Celtics	1971–1988
9	**Isiah Thomas**	3,682	Pistons	1981–1994
10	**Hakeem Olajuwon**	3,667	Rockets/Raptors	1984–2002

active player

SINGLE SEASON

1	**James Harden**	464	Rockets	2016–17
2	**Russell Westbrook**	438	Thunder	2016–17
3	**George McGinnis**	422	Pacers	1974–75
4	**George McGinnis**	401	Pacers	1972–73
5	**George McGinnis**	393	Pacers	1973–74
6	**Billy Cunningham**	381	Cougars	1972–73
	Russell Westbrook	381	Thunder	2017–18
8	**James Harden**	374	Rockets	2015–16
9	**Artis Gilmore**	366	Bulls	1977–78
10	**Ralph Simpson**	360	Nuggets	1975–76
	Kevin Porter	360	Pistons/Nets	1977–78

SINGLE GAME

1	**Jason Kidd**	14	Suns	Nov. 17, 2000	vs. Knicks
2	**Chris Mullin**	13	Warriors	Mar. 31, 1988	vs. Jazz
3	**Jason Kidd**	12	Nets	Jan. 6, 2003	vs. Hawks
	Jason Kidd	12	Nets	Mar. 16, 2003	vs. 76ers
	Allen Iverson	12	76ers	Mar. 8, 2005	vs. Warriors
	Paul Pierce	12	Celtics	Nov. 8, 2006	vs. Bobcats
	Dwyane Wade	12	Heat	Feb. 1, 2007	vs. Cavaliers
	Gilbert Arenas	12	Wizards	Nov. 10, 2009	vs. Heat
	James Harden	12	Houston	Nov. 23, 2016	vs. Raptors

▲ **Chris Mullin**

MOST TEAMS PLAYED FOR

1	**Chucky Brown**	12	1990–2002
	Tony Massenburg	12	1991–2005
	Jim Jackson	12	1993–2006
	Joe Smith	12	1996–2011
5	**Kevin Ollie**	11	1998–2010
	Mike James	11	2002–2014
7	**Mark Bryant**	10	1989–2003
	Aaron Williams	10	1994–2008
	Damon Jones	10	1999–2009
	Earl Boykins	10	1999–2012
	Drew Gooden	10	2003–2016
	Lou Amundson	10	2007–2016
	Ish Smith	10	2011–2018*

active player

RECORD FACT

A regulation NBA game is 48 minutes long. Seattle SuperSonics guard Dale Ellis holds the record for most minutes played in a single game, with 69. It happened on November 9, 1989, when his SuperSonics lost 155-154 to the Milwaukee Bucks in quintuple (five) overtime.

Games Played

1	Robert Parish	1,611	Warriors/Celtics/Hornets/Bulls	1976–1997
2	Kareem Abdul-Jabbar	1,560	Bucks/Lakers	1969–1989
3	John Stockton	1,504	Jazz	1984–2003
4	Karl Malone	1,476	Jazz/Lakers	1985–2004
5	Dirk Nowitzki	1,471	Mavericks	1998–2018*
6	Kevin Garnett	1,462	Timberwolves/Celtics/Nets	1995–2016
7	Moses Malone	1,455	Stars/Spirits/Braves/Rockets/76ers/Bullets/Hawks/Bucks/Spurs	1974–1995
8	Kevin Willis	1,424	Hawks/Heat/Warriors/Rockets/Raptors/Nuggets/Spurs/Mavericks	1984–2005, 2006–2007
9	Jason Terry	1,410	Hawks/Mavericks/Celtics/Nets/Rockets/Bucks	1999–2018*
10	Vince Carter	1,405	Raptors/Nets/Magic/Suns/Mavericks/Grizzlies/Kings	1998–2018*

active player

Minutes Played

CAREER

1	Kareem Abdul-Jabbar	57,446	Bucks/Lakers	1969–1989
2	Karl Malone	54,852	Jazz/Lakers	1985–2004
3	Dirk Nowitzki	50,573	Mavericks	1998–2018*
4	Kevin Garnett	50,418	Timberwolves/Celtics/Nets	1995–2016
5	Jason Kidd	50,111	Mavericks/Suns/Nets/Knicks	1994–2013
6	Elvin Hayes	50,000	Rockets/Bullets	1968–1984
7	Moses Malone	49,444	Stars/Spirits/Braves/Rockets/76ers/Bullets/Hawks/Bucks/Spurs	1974–1995
8	Kobe Bryant	48,637	Lakers	1996–2016
9	Wilt Chamberlain	47,859	Warriors/76ers/Lakers	1959–1973
10	John Stockton	47,764	Jazz	1984–2003

Coaches

MOST WINS

1	**Don Nelson**	1,335	Bucks/Warriors/Knicks/Mavericks	1976–2010
2	**Lenny Wilkens**	1,332	SuperSonics/Trail Blazers/Cavaliers/Hawks/Raptors/Knicks	1969–2005
3	**Larry Brown**	1,327	Cougars/Nuggets/Nets/Spurs/Clippers/Pacers/76ers/Pistons/Knicks/Bobcats	1972–2011
4	**Jerry Sloan**	1,221	Bulls/Jazz	1979–2011
5	**Pat Riley**	1,210	Lakers/Knicks/Heat	1981–2008
6	**Gregg Popovich**	1,197	Spurs	1996–2018*
7	**George Karl**	1,175	Cavaliers/Warriors/SuperSonics/Bucks/Nuggets/Kings	1984–2016
8	**Phil Jackson**	1,155	Bulls/Lakers	1989–2011
9	**Rick Adelman**	1,042	Trail Blazers/Warriors/Kings/Rockets/Timberwolves	1988–2014
10	**Bill Fitch**	944	Cavaliers/Celtics/Rockets/Nets/Clippers	1970–1998

* active coach

MOST CHAMPIONSHIPS

1	**Phil Jackson**	11
2	**Red Auerbach**	9
3	**John Kundla**	5
	Gregg Popovich	5
	Pat Riley	5
6	**Steve Kerr**	3
7	**Many coaches tied with 2**	

▲ Phil Jackson

RECORD FACT

Seven head coaches have led their team to the NBA title in their first year. Tyronn Lue was the latest to accomplish the feat. He took over as head coach of the Cleveland Cavaliers midway through the 2015–16 season, and the team went on to win the NBA title.

CHAPTER 2
Team Records

It is impossible to say which team in NBA history is the greatest. No team has dominated the game like the Boston Celtics did in the 1950s and 1960s. The Celts collected 11 NBA Championships in a 13-season stretch.

More recently, the Golden State Warriors have dominated the NBA. They have appeared in four consecutive Finals from 2015 to 2018 and won three titles. But it was the Warriors' 2015–16 season that is unmatched. The Warriors, led by superstars Steph Curry and Klay Thompson, finished the regular season with a record of 73–9. They are the only team in NBA history to lose less than ten games in a season. Though they lost in the Finals to the Cleveland Cavaliers, they are still one of the greatest teams of all time.

The question of which is the greatest team ever may not have an answer, but records help. Which team has the most titles? Which franchise has the most wins? The best teams can be found at the top of the list of the most impressive team records in the game.

Season Records

MOST WINS ALL TIME

1	Boston Celtics	3,329
2	Los Angeles Lakers	3,296
3	Philadelphia 76ers	2,806
4	New York Knicks	2,761
5	Atlanta Hawks	2,717
6	Golden State Warriors	2,715
7	Detroit Pistons	2,692
8	Sacramento Kings	2,523
9	San Antonio Spurs	2,492
10	Oklahoma City Thunder	2,234

MOST LOSSES ALL TIME

1	Sacramento Kings	3,010
2	Golden State Warriors	2,923
3	New York Knicks	2,878
4	Detroit Pistons	2,840
5	Atlanta Hawks	2,753
6	Philadelphia 76ers	2,662
7	Washington Wizards	2,519
8	Brooklyn Nets	2,358
9	Los Angeles Clippers	2,326
10	Boston Celtics	2,313

Season Records

RECORD FACT

The 2015–16 Golden State Warriors are the only team in history to play an entire season without losing two games in a row.

BEST SEASONS

1	Golden State Warriors	73–9	0.89	2015–16
2	Chicago Bulls	72–10	0.878	1995–96
3	Los Angeles Lakers	69–13	0.841	1971–72
	Chicago Bulls	69–13	0.841	1996–97
5	Philadelphia 76ers	68–13	0.84	1966–67
6	Boston Celtics	68–14	0.829	1972–73
7	Boston Celtics	67–15	0.817	1985–86
	Chicago Bulls	67–15	0.817	1991–92
	Los Angeles Lakers	67–15	0.817	1999–00
	Dallas Mavericks	67–15	0.817	2006–07
	Golden State Warriors	67–15	0.817	2014–15
	San Antonio Spurs	67–15	0.817	2015–16
	Golden State Warriors	67–15	0.817	2016–17

WORST SEASONS

1	Charlotte Bobcats	7–59	0.106	2011–12
2	Philadelphia 76ers	9–73	0.11	1972–73
3	Philadelphia 76ers	10–72	0.122	2015–16
4	Providence Steam Rollers	6–42	0.125	1947–48
5	Dallas Mavericks	11–71	0.134	1992–93
	Denver Nuggets	11–71	0.134	1997–98
7	Los Angeles Clippers	12–70	0.146	1986–87
	New Jersey Nets	12–70	0.146	2009–10
9	Dallas Mavericks	13–69	0.159	1993–94
	Atlanta Hawks	13–69	0.159	2004–05

▲ Charlotte Bobcats

LONGEST WINNING STREAK

1	Los Angeles Lakers	33	1971–72
2	Golden State Warriors	28	2014–15, 2015–16
3	Miami Heat	27	2012–13
4	Houston Rockets	22	2007–08
5	Washington Capitols	20	1947–48, 1948–49
	Milwaukee Bucks	20	1970–71
7	Los Angeles Lakers	19	1999–00
	Boston Celtics	19	2008–09
	San Antonio Spurs	19	2013–14
	Atlanta Hawks	19	2014–15

LONGEST LOSING STREAK

1	Philadelphia 76ers	28	2014–15, 2015–16
2	Cleveland Cavaliers	26	2010–11
	Philadelphia 76ers	26	2013–14
4	Cleveland Cavaliers	24	1981–82, 1982–83
5	Vancouver Grizzlies	23	1995–96
	Denver Nuggets	23	1997–98
	Charlotte Bobcats	23	2011–12
8	Detroit Pistons	21	1979–80, 1980–81
9	Philadelphia 76ers	20	1972–73
	New York Knicks	20	1984–85, 1985–86
	Dallas Mavericks	20	1993–94
	Los Angeles Clippers	20	1993–94, 1994–95

RECORD FACT

The New York Knicks hold the record for longest losing streak in the playoffs. They lost 13 straight postseason games over 11 seasons.

41

CHAPTER 3
Playoff Records

It doesn't matter how great a team is during the regular season if they don't perform in the playoffs. The Golden State Warriors learned that lesson. In 2015–16, the Warriors dominated the NBA, recording a historical 73–9 record. Unfortunately, when the playoffs came, Steph Curry, Draymond Green, and the rest of the Warriors ran out of gas, losing the title to the Cleveland Cavaliers in seven games.

How did the Warriors respond? They returned in 2016 and delivered the greatest playoff run in the history of the game. The Warriors added superstar Kevin Durant during the offseason. Alongside Steph Curry, Klay Thompson, and Draymond Green, the "Fantastic Four" rolled up a 16–1 record in the playoffs.

Great seasons are important. But as the 2016–17 Golden State Warriors learned, it isn't how you start, it's how you finish. Their dominant playoff run included winning 15 straight games and earning the franchise its fifth NBA Championship.

MOST NBA TITLES

1	Bill Russell	11
2	Sam Jones	10
3	John Havlicek	8
	Tom Heinsohn	8
	K.C. Jones	8
	Tom Sanders	8
7	Robert Horry	7
	Frank Ramsey	7
9	Kareem Abdul-Jabbar	6
	Bob Cousy	6
	Michael Jordan	6
	Jim Loscutoff	6
	Scottie Pippen	6

Playoff Records

MOST PLAYOFF GAMES PLAYED

1	Derek Fisher	259
2	Tim Duncan	251
3	Robert Horry	244
4	LeBron James	239*
5	Kareem Abdul-Jabbar	237
6	Tony Parker	226*
7	Kobe Bryant	220
8	Manu Ginobili	218*
9	Shaquille O'Neal	216
10	Scottie Pippen	208

▲ Derek Fisher

MOST NBA FINALS MVP AWARDS

1	Michael Jordan	6
2	Tim Duncan	3
	LeBron James	3*
	Magic Johnson	3
	Shaquille O'Neal	3
6	Kareem Abdul-Jabbar	2
	Larry Bird	2
	Kobe Bryant	2
	Kevin Durant	2
	Hakeem Olajuwon	2
	Willis Reed	2

active player

▲ Kevin Durant

Playoff Points

▲ LeBron James

CAREER

1	LeBron James	6,911*
2	Michael Jordan	5,987
3	Kareem Abdul-Jabbar	5,762
4	Kobe Bryant	5,640
5	Shaquille O'Neal	5,250
6	Tim Duncan	5,172
7	Karl Malone	4,761
8	Julius Erving	4,580
9	Jerry West	4,457
10	Tony Parker	4,045*

active player

SINGLE GAME

1	Michael Jordan	63	Bulls	Apr. 20, 1986
2	Elgin Baylor	61	Lakers	Apr. 14, 1962
3	Wilt Chamberlain	56	Warriors	Mar. 22, 1962
	Michael Jordan	56	Bulls	Apr. 29, 1992
	Charles Barkley	56	Suns	May 4, 1994
6	Rick Barry	55	Warriors	Apr. 18, 1967
	Michael Jordan	55	Bulls	May 1, 1988
	Michael Jordan	55	Bulls	June 16, 1993
	Michael Jordan	55	Bulls	Apr. 27, 1997
	Allen Iverson	55	76ers	Apr. 20, 2003

RECORD FACT

It took Michael Jordan two overtimes to set his 63-point playoff record. It came in a double-overtime against the Boston Celtics on April 20, 1986. Unfortunately, the Bulls lost the game, 135-131.

Playoff Rebounds

CAREER

1	Bill Russell	4,104
2	Wilt Chamberlain	3,913
3	Tim Duncan	2,859
4	Shaquille O'Neal	2,508
5	Kareem Abdul-Jabbar	2,481
6	LeBron James	2,122
7	Karl Malone	2,062
8	Wes Unseld	1,777
9	Robert Parish	1,765
10	Elgin Baylor	1,724

▲ Karl Malone

SINGLE GAME

1	Wilt Chamberlain	41	76ers	Apr. 5, 1967
2	Bill Russell	40	Celtics	Mar. 23, 1958
	Bill Russell	40	Celtics	Mar. 29, 1960
	Bill Russell	40	Celtics	Apr. 18, 1962
5	Bill Russell	39	Celtics	Mar. 19, 1960
	Bill Russell	39	Celtics	Mar. 23, 1961
	Wilt Chamberlain	39	76ers	Apr. 6, 1965
8	Bill Russell	38	Celtics	Apr. 11, 1961
	Bill Russell	38	Celtics	Apr. 16, 1963
	Wilt Chamberlain	38	Warriors	Apr. 24, 1964

RECORD FACT

Bill Russell and Wilt Chamberlain each averaged 24 rebounds per game for their playoff careers. The third highest career rebounder, Tim Duncan, averaged just 11.4 per game.

Playoff Assists

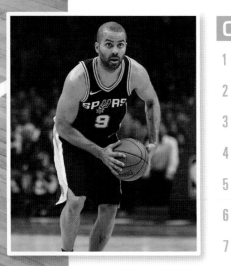

▲ Tony Parker

CAREER

1	Magic Johnson	2,346
2	John Stockton	1,839
3	LeBron James	1,687*
4	Jason Kidd	1,263
5	Tony Parker	1,143*
6	Larry Bird	1,062
7	Steve Nash	1,061
8	Scottie Pippen	1,048
9	Kobe Bryant	1,040
10	Michael Jordan	1,022

SINGLE GAME

1	Magic Johnson	24	Lakers	May 15, 1984
	John Stockton	24	Jazz	May 17, 1988
3	Magic Johnson	23	Lakers	May 3, 1985
	John Stockton	23	Jazz	Apr. 25, 1996
	Steve Nash	23	Suns	Apr. 29, 2007
6	Doc Rivers	22	Hawks	May 16, 1988
7	Magic Johnson	21	Lakers	June 3, 1984
	Magic Johnson	21	Lakers	Apr. 27, 1991
	Magic Johnson	21	Lakers	May 18, 1991
	John Stockton	21	Jazz	Apr. 24, 1992
	Rajon Rondo	21	Pelicans	May 4, 2018*

** stats begin in 1984

Playoff 3-Pointers

CAREER

1	Ray Allen	385
2	Stephen Curry	378*
3	LeBron James	370*
4	Manu Ginobili	324*
5	Reggie Miller	320
6	Klay Thompson	304*
7	Kobe Bryant	292
8	J.R. Smith	288*
9	Derek Fisher	285
10	Paul Pierce	276

▲ Ray Allen

SINGLE GAME

1	Klay Thompson	11	Warriors	May 28, 2016*
2	Rex Chapman	9	Suns	Apr. 25, 1997
	Vince Carter	9	Raptors	May 11, 2001*
	Ray Allen	9	Bucks	June 1, 2001
	Ray Allen	9	Celtics	Apr. 30, 2009
	Jason Terry	9	Mavericks	May 8, 2011*
	Klay Thompson	9	Warriors	May 26, 2018*
	Stephen Curry	9	Warriors	June 3, 2018*
9	Many players tied with 8			

* active player

RECORD FACT

Stephen Curry of the Golden State Warriors holds the record for most three-point shots made in an NBA Finals game. Curry knocked down nine for 27 points against the Cleveland Cavaliers on June 3, 2018.

Playoff Steals

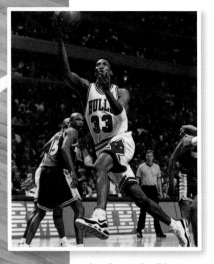

▲ Scottie Pippen

	CAREER	
1	LeBron James	419*
2	Scottie Pippen	395
3	Michael Jordan	376
4	Magic Johnson	358
5	John Stockton	338
6	Kobe Bryant	310
7	Jason Kidd	302
8	Larry Bird	296
9	Maurice Cheeks	295
10	Manu Ginobili	292*

active player

AILING AIR JORDAN

There have been many heroic performances in the NBA playoffs through the years. Michael Jordan has offered up several of the biggest. Jordan's best may have come in Game 5 of the 1997 Finals against the Utah Jazz. Jordan was suffering from the flu. He was dizzy, dehydrated, and sick the entire game. But the series was tied at two games apiece, and his team was on the road. Jordan couldn't quit, so he fought through and delivered 38 points and a win for his team. After the game, Jordan's coach, Phil Jackson, called it "a heroic effort, one to add to the collection of efforts that make up his legend."

CHAMPIONSHIPS

1	Boston Celtics	17
2	Los Angeles Lakers	16
3	Chicago Bulls	6
	Golden State Warriors	6
5	San Antonio Spurs	5
6	Detroit Pistons	3
	Indiana Pacers	3
	Miami Heat	3
	Philadelphia 76ers	3

▲ Boston Celtics, 2008

YEARS IN THE PLAYOFFS

1	Los Angeles Lakers	60
2	Boston Celtics	55
3	Philadelphia 76ers	48
4	Atlanta Hawks	46
	San Antonio Spurs	46
6	New York Knicks	42
7	Detroit Pistons	41
8	Chicago Bulls	35
9	Golden State Warriors	34
	Indiana Pacers	34
	Portland Trail Blazers	34

RECORD FACT

The San Antonio Spurs have appeared in the playoffs for 21 consecutive seasons (1998–2018).

CHAPTER 4
The All-Star Game

The NBA All-Star Game is a chance for fans to see the game's greatest players all on the court at the same time. The game is usually high-scoring as the best in the game show off their high-flying offensive skills. But the All-Star Game is more than a single game. It includes a weekend of competition before the game.

The Slam Dunk Contest gives players a chance to show how high they can fly. Players have leaped over other players, mascots, and even over cars before delivering a dazzling dunk.

Then there is the three-point con The game's elite long-range shooters are given 60 seconds to drain as man 3-pointers as they can. In 1991, Chic Bulls guard Craig Hodges knocked down 19 consecutive shots in less tha minute to win the trophy. It is an acti packed atmosphere for the fans and s the stage for the big game.

All-Star Records

ALL-STAR SELECTIONS

1	Kareem Abdul-Jabbar	19
	Kobe Bryant	18
3	Julius Erving	16
4	Tim Duncan	15
	Kevin Garnett	15
	Shaquille O'Neal	15
7	LeBron James	14
	Michael Jordan	14
	Karl Malone	14
	Jerry West	14

CAREER POINTS

1	LeBron James	343*
2	Kobe Bryant	290
3	Michael Jordan	262

CAREER ASSISTS

1	Magic Johnson	127
2	Chris Paul	106*
3	Isiah Thomas	97

active player

CAREER REBOUNDS

1	Wilt Chamberlain	197
2	Bob Pettit	178
3	Kareem Abdul-Jabbar	149

CAREER STEALS

1	Kobe Bryant	38
2	Michael Jordan	37
3	Isiah Thomas	31

CAREER BLOCKS

1	Kareem Abdul-Jabbar	31
2	Hakeem Olajuwon	23
3	Shaquille O'Neal	19

▲ Shaquille O'Neal

RECORD FACT

The 2016 West All-Stars set the record for most points scored in an All-Star Game, with 196. They topped the East, 196-173.

All-Star Records

▲ Allen Iverson

MULTIPLE ALL-STAR GAME MVP AWARDS

1	Bob Pettit	4	1956, 1958, 1959, 1962
	Kobe Bryant	4	2002, 2007, 2009, 2011
3	Oscar Robertson	3	1961, 1964, 1969
	Michael Jordan	3	1988, 1996, 1998
	Shaquille O'Neal	3	2000, 2004, 2009
	LeBron James	3	2006, 2008, 2018
7	Bob Cousy	2	1954, 1957
	Julius Erving	2	1977, 1983
	Isiah Thomas	2	1984, 1986
	Karl Malone	2	1989, 1993
	Magic Johnson	2	1990, 1992
	Allen Iverson	2	2001, 2005

SUPER SPUD

The NBA is considered a tall man's league, but don't tell that to Anthony "Spud" Webb. Though he was only 5 feet 7 inches (170 cm) tall, Webb could jump. He beat out the best in the NBA to win the 1986 Slam Dunk Contest during the NBA All-Star Game.

▲ Spud Webb

MULTIPLE SLAM DUNK CONTEST WINNERS

1	Nate Robinson	3	Knicks	2006, 2009, 2010
2	Dominique Wilkins	2	Hawks	1985, 1990
	Michael Jordan	2	Bulls	1987, 1988
	Harold Miner	2	Heat	1993, 1995
	Jason Richardson	2	Warriors	2002, 2003
	Zach LaVine	2	Timberwolves	2015, 2016*

▲ Nate Robinson

MULTIPLE 3-POINT SHOOTOUT WINNERS

1	Larry Bird	3	1986, 1987, 1988
	Craig Hodges	3	1990, 1991, 1992
3	Mark Price	2	1993, 1994
	Jeff Hornacek	2	1998, 2000
	Peja Stojakovic	2	2002, 2003
	Jason Kapono	2	2007, 2008

▲ Larry Bird

RECORD FACT

Kobe Bryant was named to the All-Star Game in 18 of his 20 seasons in the NBA, winning the MVP award four times.

CHAPTER 5

The WNBA

On June 17, 2017, history was made in Los Angeles. With her team down nearly 20 points to the host Sparks, Phoenix Mercury guard Diana Taurasi brought the ball up court. With one quick move, she drove to the basket and banked a soft layup off the glass and in. It didn't change the outcome of the game. However, it gave Taurasi 7,489 career points, making her the all-time leading scorer in Women's National Basketball Association (WNBA) history.

Since it was launched in 1997, the WNBA has showcased the talent of some incredible athletes. Early pioneers of the league, like Lisa Leslie and Rebecca Lobo, set the table for today's superstars to shine. Before the WNBA, women had to go overseas if they wanted to continue playing basketball after college. Now, they play before adoring crowds in Los Angeles, Chicago, New York, Atlanta, and across the United States. Young stars like Angel McCoughtry, Tina Charles, and Tiffany Hayes blend with veterans like Taurasi to give fans a competitive brand of basketball every night.

It may only be 22 years old, but the WNBA has already established an impressive list of records. These are sure to grow as the league continues to develop the best of the best on the hardwood.

Points

CAREER

1	**Diana Taurasi**	7,867	Mercury	2004–2017*
2	**Tina Thompson**	7,488	Comets/Sparks/Storm	1997–2013
3	**Tamika Catchings**	7,380	Fever	2002–2016
4	**Cappie Pondexter**	6,591	Mercury/Liberty/Sky/Sparks	2006–2017*
5	**Katie Smith**	6,452	Lynx/Shock/Mystics/Storm/Liberty	1999–2013
6	**Lisa Leslie**	6,263	Sparks	1997–2009
7	**Lauren Jackson**	6,007	Storm	2001–2012
8	**Becky Hammon**	5,841	Liberty/Silver Stars	1999–2014
9	**Sue Bird**	5,840	Storm	2002–2017*
10	**Candice Dupree**	5,602	Sky/Mercury/Fever	2006–2017*

▲ Tina Thompson

SINGLE SEASON

1	**Diana Taurasi**	860	Mercury	2006*
2	**Diana Taurasi**	820	Mercury	2008*
3	**Maya Moore**	812	Lynx	2014
4	**Seimone Augustus**	769	Lynx	2007*
5	**Seimone Augustus**	744	Lynx	2006*
6	**Katie Smith**	739	Lynx	2001
	Lauren Jackson	739	Storm	2007
8	**Cappie Pondexter**	729	Liberty	2010*
9	**Elena Delle Donne**	725	Sky	2015*
10	**Angel McCoughtry**	716	Dream	2010*

▲ Maya Moore

* active player **all WNBA stats and records are through the 2017 season

Points

SINGLE GAME

1	Riquna Williams	51	Shock	Sept. 8, 2013*
2	Maya Moore	48	Lynx	July 22, 2014*
3	Diana Taurasi	47	Mercury	Aug. 10, 2006*

MULTIPLE MVP WINNERS

1	Sheryl Swoopes	3	2000, 2002, 2005
	Lisa Leslie	3	2001, 2004, 2006
	Lauren Jackson	3	2003, 2007, 2010
4	Cynthia Cooper	2	1997, 1998
5	Candace Parker	2	2008, 2013

active player

▲ Sheryl Swoopes

3-Pointers

CAREER

1	Diana Taurasi	996	Mercury	2004–2017*
2	Katie Smith	906	Lynx/Shock/Mystics/Storm/Liberty	1999–2013
3	Becky Hammon	829	Liberty/Silver Stars	1999–2014
4	Sue Bird	795	Storm	2002–2017*
5	Tina Thompson	748	Comets/Sparks/Storm	1997–2013
6	Katie Douglas	726	Miracle/Sun/Fever	2001–2014
7	Tamika Catchings	606	Fever	2002–2016
8	Kara Lawson	584	Monarchs/Sun/Mystics	2003–2015
9	Nicole Powell	580	Sting/Monarchs/Liberty/Shock/Storm	2004–2014
10	Ivory Latta	536	Shock/Dream/Mystics	2007–2017

▲ Katie Smith

SINGLE SEASON

1	Diana Taurasi	121	Mercury	2006*
2	Diana Taurasi	96	Mercury	2017*
3	Diana Taurasi	95	Mercury	2007*
4	Diana Taurasi	89	Mercury	2008*
	Diana Taurasi	89	Mercury	2016*
6	Katie Smith	88	Lynx	2000
7	Sugar Rodgers	86	Liberty	2016*
8	Katie Smith	85	Lynx	2001
9	Diana Taurasi	81	Mercury	2011*
	Ivory Latta	81	Mystics	2014
	Kristi Toliver	81	Sparks	2016*

active player

▲ Kristi Toliver

Assists

▲ Sue Bird

CAREER

1	**Sue Bird**	2,610	Storm	2002–2017*
2	**Ticha Penicheiro**	2,599	Monarchs/Sparks/Sky	1998–2012
3	**Lindsay Whalen**	2,246	Sun/Lynx	2004–2017*
4	**Becky Hammon**	1,708	Liberty/Silver Stars	1999–2014
5	**Diana Taurasi**	1,659	Mercury	2004–2017*
6	**Cappie Pondexter**	1,524	Mercury/Liberty/Sky/Sparks	2006–2017*
7	**Tamika Catchings**	1,488	Fever	2002–2016
8	**Shannon Johnson**	1,424	Miracle/Sun/Silver Stars/Shock/Comets/Storm	1999–2009
9	**Temeka Johnson**	1,382	Mystics/Sparks/Mercury/Shock/Storm	2005–2015
10	**Teresa Weatherspoon**	1,338	Liberty/Sparks	1997–2004

SINGLE SEASON

1	**Ticha Penicheiro**	236	Monarchs	2000
2	**Ticha Penicheiro**	229	Monarchs	2003
3	**Ticha Penicheiro**	226	Monarchs	1999
	Layshia Clarendon	226	Dream	2017*
5	**Ticha Penicheiro**	224	Monarchs	1998
6	**Sue Bird**	221	Storm	2003*
7	**Ticha Penicheiro**	220	Sparks	2010
8	**Courtney Vandersloot**	218	Sky	2017*
9	**Nikki Teasley**	214	Sparks	2003
10	**Nikki Teasley**	207	Sparks	2004

* active player

Rebounds

CAREER

1	**Tamika Catchings**	3,316	Fever	2002–2016
2	**Lisa Leslie**	3,307	Sparks	1997–2009
3	**Rebekkah Brunson**	3,186	Monarchs/Lynx	2004–2017*
4	**Tina Thompson**	3,070	Comets/Sparks./Storm	1997–2013
5	**Taj McWilliams-Franklin**	3,013	Miracle/Sun/Sparks/Mystics/Shock/Liberty/Lynx	1999–2012
6	**Tina Charles**	2,653	Sun/Liberty	2010–2017*
7	**Sylvia Fowles**	2,626	Sky/Lynx	2008–2017*
8	**DeLisha Milton-Jones**	2,574	Sparks/Mystics/Silver Stars/Liberty/Dream	1999–2015
9	**Candice Dupree**	2,569	Sky/Mercury/Fever	2006–2017*
10	**Swin Cash**	2,521	Shock/Storm/Sky/Dream/Liberty	2002–2016

SINGLE SEASON

1	**Jonquel Jones**	403	Sun	2017*
2	**Tina Charles**	398	Sun	2010*
3	**Tina Charles**	374	Sun	2011*
4	**Sylvia Fowles**	369	Sky	2013*
5	**Cheryl Ford**	363	Shock	2006
6	**Yolanda Griffith**	357	Monarchs	2001
7	**Sylvia Fowles**	354	Lynx	2017
8	**Sylvia Fowles**	347	Sky	2011*
	Courtney Paris	347	Shock	2014*
10	**Tina Charles**	345	Sun	2012*

active player

▲ Jonquel Jones

Steals

▲ Tamika Catchings

CAREER

1	**Tamika Catchings**	1,074	Fever	2002–2016
2	**Ticha Penicheiro**	764	Monarchs/Sparks/Sky	1998–2012
3	**Sheryl Swoopes**	657	Comets/Storm/Shock	1997–2000, 2002–2008, 2011
4	**Alana Beard**	653	Mystics/Sparks	2004–2017*
5	**Jia Perkins**	635	Sting/Sky/Silver Stars/Lynx	2004–2017
6	**Katie Douglas**	623	Miracle/Sun/Fever	2001–2014
7	**DeLisha Milton-Jones**	619	Sparks/Mystics/Silver Stars/Liberty/Dream	1999–2015
8	**Sue Bird**	617	Storm	2002–2017*
9	**Sancho Lyttle**	605	Comets/Dream/Mercury	2005–2017*
10	**Taj McWilliams-Franklin**	580	Miracle/Sun/Sparks/Mystic/Shock/Liberty/Lynx	1999–2012

▲ Teresa Weatherspoon

SINGLE SEASON

1	**Teresa Weatherspoon**	100	Liberty	1998
2	**Tamika Catchings**	99	Fever	2009
3	**Tamika Catchings**	94	Fever	2002
	Tamika Catchings	94	Fever	2006
5	**Tamika Catchings**	90	Fever	2005
6	**Angel McCoughtry**	89	Dream	2013*
7	**Sheryl Swoopes**	88	Comets	2002
8	**Sheryl Swoopes**	87	Comets	2000
9	**Teresa Weatherspoon**	85	Liberty	1997
	Tamika Catchings	85	Fever	2013

active player

Blocks

CAREER

1	**Margo Dydek**	877	Starzz/Silver Stars/ Sun/Sparks	1998–2008
2	**Lisa Leslie**	822	Sparks	1997–2009
3	**Lauren Jackson**	586	Storm	2001–2012
4	**Tangela Smith**	557	Monarchs/Sting/Mercury/ Fever/Silver Stars	1998–2012
5	**Tammy Sutton-Brown**	555	Sting/Fever	2001–2012
6	**Sylvia Fowles**	530	Sky/Lynx	2008–2017*
7	**Ruth Riley**	505	Sol/Shock/Silver Stars/Sky/Dream	2001–2013
8	**Brittney Griner**	487	Mercury	2013–2017*
9	**Candace Parker**	468	Sparks	2008–2017*
10	**Taj McWilliams-Franklin**	443	Miracle/Sun/Sparks/ Mystic/Shock/Liberty/Lynx	1999–2012

▲ Margo Dydek

SINGLE SEASON

1	**Brittney Griner**	129	Mercury	2014
2	**Margo Dydek**	114	Starzz	1998
3	**Margo Dydek**	113	Starzz	2001
4	**Margo Dydek**	107	Starzz	2002
	Brittney Griner	107	Mercury	2016
6	**Brittney Griner**	105	Mercury	2015
7	**Margo Dydek**	100	Silver Stars	2003
8	**Lisa Leslie**	98	Sparks	2004
9	**Lisa Leslie**	97	Sparks	2008
10	**Margo Dydek**	96	Starzz	2000

* active player

▲ Brittney Griner

Read More

Adamson, Thomas K. *Basketball Records.* Incredible Sports Records. Minneapolis, Minn.: Bellwether Media, Inc., 2018.

Chandler, Matt. *Wacky Basketball Trivia.* North Mankato, Minn.: Capstone Press, 2017.

Frederick, Shane. *Basketball's Record Breakers.* North Mankato, Minn.: Capstone Press, 2017.

Internet Sites

Use FactHound to find Internet sites related to this book.

Visit *www.facthound.com*

Just type in 9781543554601 and go.

 **Super-cool stuff!** Check out projects, games and lots more at
www.capstonekids.com

Index